# *Power of a 1000 Suns*

## *(a poetry book)*

Jameel Baker

*"I have the power
to be fine.
I have the power
to be divine.
The power to evolve
myself,
time after time.
And I wield this power,
for me,
 all mine."*

# *Author's Message:*

  Self-evolution is not just a process; it's a profound gift bestowed upon us. It ignites a beautiful revolution within, capable of transforming us into the very best versions of ourselves. This remarkable journey knows no boundaries, it transcends and blazes with an intensity that is both invigorating and unstoppable. It possesses a raw power that cannot be contained, an inexorable force that propels us towards boundless self-growth, where we acknowledge our strengths and shortcomings, while learning to accept and grow with them.

  Within the pages of this collection lies a testament to this transformative power. It is a poignant chronicle capturing glimpses of my personal evolution—a candid exploration of my unfiltered and authentic moments. In times of growth, renewal, betterment, and new beginnings, I found myself documenting my journey, giving voice to the depths of my intuition and thoughts.

  Throughout my travels across Asia, I sought inspiration in diverse settings and unfamiliar surroundings. I wrote in many different places and environments. I met strangers and took new risks. I experienced beautiful smiles, spontaneous decisions, long nights filled with laughter and inspiration, and profound moments of rediscovery. I enjoyed the winds of Bangkok and its breathtaking sunsets and sunrises. Hiked and rode a motorcycle in Pai, listened to the stories from the locals of Chiang Mai, got lost in Kowloon, prayed for 16 hours in Bulacan, coasted along Ha Long Bay in solitude, practiced gratitude in Bukit Timah, and soaked up the serenity of the Pearl River Delta.

  All of these instances inspired me to document rising emotions, thoughts, and distant memories. Every moment of joy, love, confusion, grief, heartbreak, and uncertainty, it all spoke to me. It told me to write. Not with the direct intention that this would become something to share or a work of art, but rather it was a means of expression, a conduit for my innermost self. In transforming these sensations into words, and transcribing those words onto paper, I engaged in an act of personal alchemy, birthing something entirely pure and uniquely mine.

  May this collection inspire moments of clarity and transparency within you, as it did with me. I hope these words form a connection with you, even if it's just a head nod. I hope my words reflecting myself, inspires you to be more of who you are, and not who you think you are. May it embolden you to embark upon a journey of courage and self-exploration. Above all, I hope that this collection reminds you of the unspoken truths that reside within you, or the things you don't give voice to, in hopes that you do.

With gratitude,

Jameel Baker [@penprophet]

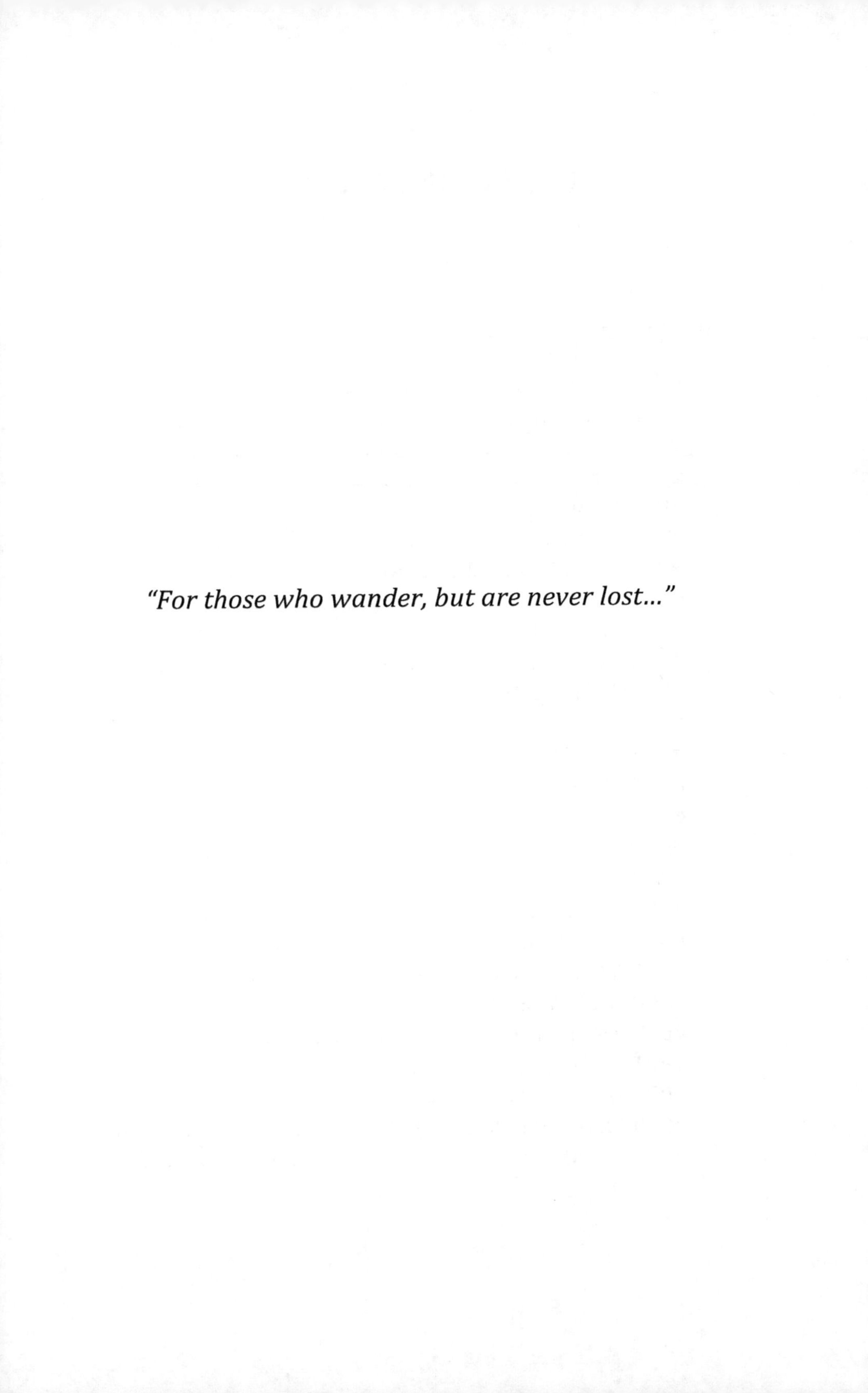

*"For those who wander, but are never lost..."*

# TABLE OF CONTENTS

# PROPHECY BOY

*(IT WAS WRITTEN)*

# #BROKEN.STRENGTH

We find strength
often when
we are
broken
and
direction
when
we
are
lost...

# #MEELY

On a quest for acceptance,
they had to say goodbye to the things
they once knew to be true.
So,
they fell into a deep sleep,
one they thought would keep them free
and the people happy.

And when they woke up,
there was no one around.
No one to care.
No muse,
as the people all carried on with their usual ways:
routine-like,
with no real knack for individuality or
expression as part of their daily appetite.
And yet,
the goal they kept for so
long,
was the same goal
that made
the pain prolong.

The goal of wanting to be
part of something great,
was the same goal
that only served disappointment,
and continually led them
to their demised fate.
And now hating this game,
which they have been destined to
play for as long as they can
remember,
they set out to try again.
The game of chasing acceptance
in places they
know, or left behind,
and even
have been.

And when the days turn to
months and the months
mature
into years,
causing them to
lose track of time
and never fully realizing
that a
lack of acceptance
was their
primary fear,
they
altered who they were,
believing it was all meant to
change.
Believing that,
in life,

nothing remains the same...

You see,

they both stared
at their scars
and realized
sometimes old habits
bring new pains,
and these reminders
always will feel the
same, no matter how the
wounds have
healed and no longer
bleed of disdain!

The things they
wanted to keep
were subject to judgement,
and deemed useless.
They would not bring them any fame.
A hard
revelation in a losing game.

So,
acceptance sends them out on
a spiral again and again.
Never knowing life outside of the goal of
acceptance.
Vowing to never return to a
life
that is in full pursuit
of
rejection...

# #MIRACLE

Even with such
    tears,
    you're still the
    most beautiful gem.
    I never knew
    pain
    could
    look so beautiful
    with
    water flowing like art
    from your eyes...

# #REASON

This pen writes
to reason.
To encompass
spaces
with the intention of feeling.
It writes to overcome
and
create room for healing.

# #UNTITLED

A work of art
that
is
free...
Now
that's
a life
that is
meant
for me...

# #HERCULES

He was unstoppable.
Born with a firm grip
and
a skin so thick,
but that didn't
stop what
killed him from within.

Who knew
that the silent
heartaches
break
even
the strongest of men
in two!
No words
to substitute
for glue...

# #EXCELLENCE VS PERFECTION

True perfection
is not the polished
and well put together view,
but rather the struggle to
express something true.

Look for these moments
and not a distorted
'perfect' view.
Perfection is messy too!

# #UNTITLED

Being the best
doesn't have
a distinct face.
But being
YOU
does
and that
is enough...

# #S.E.Q.U.E.N.C.E

        To proceed over
    or to hide under,
        a constant dance to overcome...
        Identical forces
        summoned by decisions
    that
        forge a path
         towards
        becoming
        one...

# #R.O.A.R

Dear worries,
worry me no more.

I am standing tall
without fears.

Vulnerable.
Open.

Shining
with a freedom
that sings
across even
the deafest
of
ears.

Here me
roar
some more
as I
drop
 all these
worries
to the floor...

# #PRACTICE MODESTY

Do not
give up
on
people
who are
incomplete…

That includes you too…

# #VIPER

He came into
a world
where people lack vision.
He
only

knew

what they could

not
see...

# #HOPELESS EYES
## (undying love)
*- a haiku*

Lonely eyes still cry.

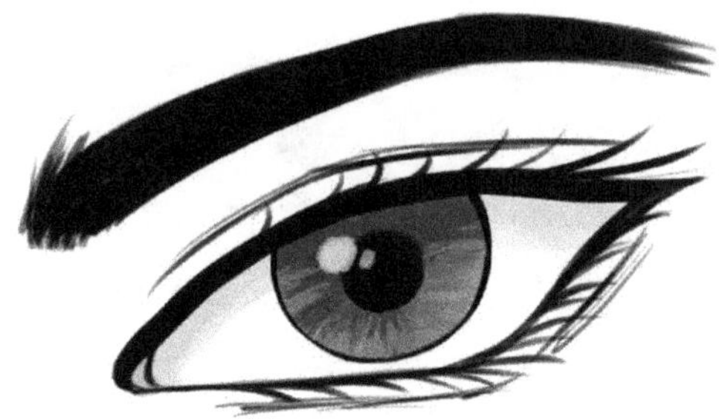

Even after all this time.
What's alive can't die...

# #UNTITLED

Sometimes the mind
must break
for the soul
to open...

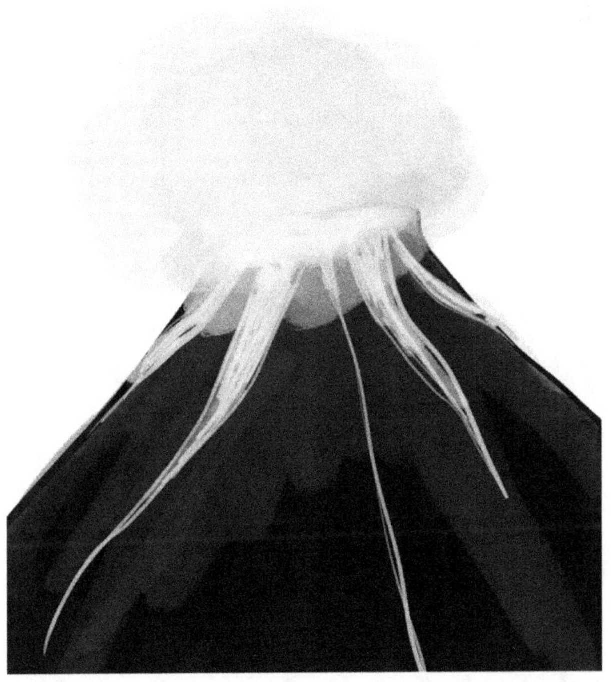

# #YOU

It was there all along,
with every smile
and every frown.
It was there all along,
with every truth and every cry.
In the far corner where he stayed,
in the background
where no one notices the
things that tend to fade.


It was there.


He was there…

# #D.I.Y

What a design in the
mirror today!
Feeling
renewed, feeling
alive. Growing to be
so bold

and yet,
deteriorating
in every moment in time...
And just when you think
nothing is left,
what has been
there
all along
begins to shine...

# #加油

(jiā yóu)

That's duality
I suppose,
you learn from the highs
and lows,
some wins,
some woes....

# #TRANSGRESS!

Aren't we fortunate enough
to know that when
the mind is lost,
the heart will lead the way.
And when the
heart is blind,
the soul saves the day?

We have all we need,
every step of the way!
The answer lies within,
until you fade away.

Tell a friend.

What happened to you?
"I" happened...

# #ANGEL TEARS

And I
knew
angels hurt too,
when I saw
the most
beautiful cry.

- divine tears from the most
captivating of eyes...

# #UNTITLED

They say it is
hard to love
with no one around,
but loving
yourself,
now that's
profound!
A love that
is full,
whole,
and
round...

# #ACQUIRED TASTE

You were the
right kind
of bad,
in a world
full of
good
and disaster...

# #LIGHTNING AND GOLIATH

I was
the storm
and you were
the sky…

A
catastrophe
brewing,
where only the
two of us
could
survive…

The two of us,
you and I,
to witness each
other
and thrive…

# #POTENTIAL

And maybe
we suppress
the best parts of us.
The parts we don't believe
                or
the parts that we internalize
and
think to call

bluff.

But this is YOU!
Wonderfully magnificent too!
If only you knew how
unique you are.
Only if you believed your heart
to feel what is truly you!
And accept it to be true!

Surely YOU can be
able and
capable
too!

# #BROKEN-OPEN
### (version 3)

And with breaking,
something new must emerge.
Something beautiful is bound
to
be...
Broken,
sure,
but never broken
truly,
rather
opening to be

free...
Broken open
solely to release
me...

# #CIRCLE OF LIFE (KARMA)

It's morning.


The early
rays of
sunrise
mark
my first conscious
breath of the day.

It can mark another rebirth
and
a new
day serving life,
while being cursed in a cycle
of little
deaths.

And they say with each breath,
little by little,
moment to moment,
we are one step closer to death.


So live today!

# #A BOY CRIED BLACK
## (version 2)

In hopes that I
may move forward,
I must let go of the
hopes and regrets
I hold for changing
things left
in the past.

Made up of
what if...

or should I...

or perhaps...

or maybe...

or
should have...

I have my own reasons and demons.
Lies and truths that arrive at certain seasons.

And sometimes I feel like it takes time
to be great,
especially during the times I feel like
nothing at all.

While for others it seems
easy,
like they were destined from birth,
no failure sealed in their fate, no fall.
But I hold on to the hope that
one day
I
too can forever stand
tall.

Always
stuck between
two different worlds:

Being and becoming...

# BEING AND BECOMING

# #LOVE HURTS
# (LEVEL 1)

Between the truths
and lies,
their hearts
had always
played
the
love
game
very
wise...

# #WHO KNOWS?

When my mind
happens to wander
to you,
are these the moments
when you think
of me too?

Do you still think
of the way
my eyes made
love
to parts
that you never knew?

Irreplaceable...

# #<3

Real love
is so much
more
than just words...

# #ALIVE&COMPLEX

I once was a broken fix,
made up of
promises left on
virgin ears.

Only knowing of
a pain that cuts
thin and deep.

A complex combination
inside of me.
Creating a world of chaos,
where only walls that
keep me together
can only withstand.

A combination where ends
don't meet
and the only resolve,
is an unspeakable pain,
resulting in  an all too familiar defeat.

A beautiful tale
of what
I once was,
and as I breathe in new life,
it is faith that reminds me
that my heart
continues to beat...

# #JACKTHERIPPER

She pulled me out
of something
I never knew
I was lost in.
An abyss
toying with my
vision,
as emotions
wore me
thin...

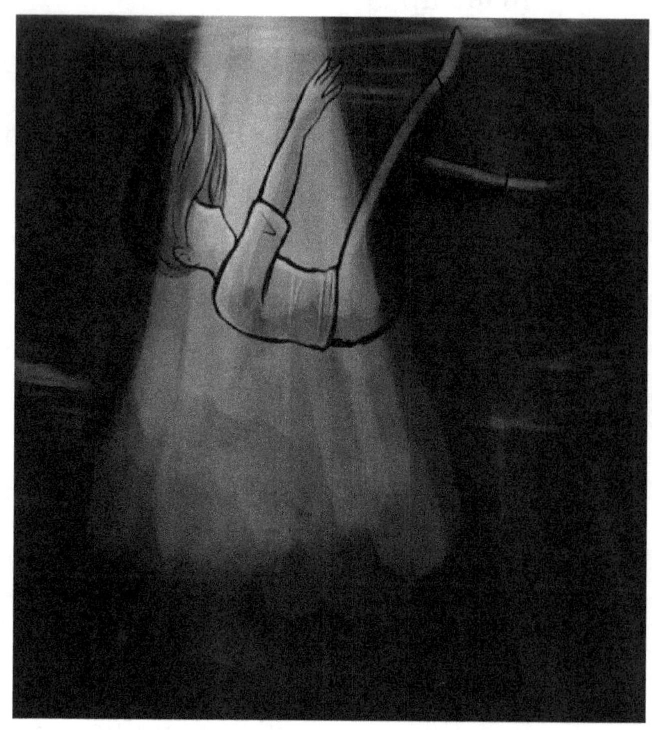

# #SLUMBER

I am asleep in the depths
of your eyes.
I
am
beautifully
entranced,
    and I don't
dare
to
wake...

# #TABULA RASA

So much heartbreak
for such a
small heart.

No wonder
you
don't
know
how
to love,
    or
be loved...

# #GENESIS (CREATION)

A
dimension
shaped by your love,
is the only reality
I want to be lost
in.


Until time do us part...

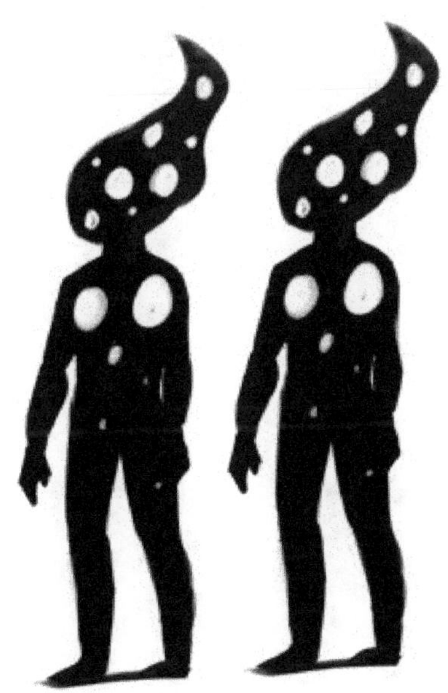

# #A HAND-MADE TALE

Were
we
forged
by the
hands
   of
an angel,
just to become
such hideous
creations?

Difference was my strength!

# #JUBILATION

You said that
I
lost
the moment I left.
Truth of the matter is
I
was always
the prize...

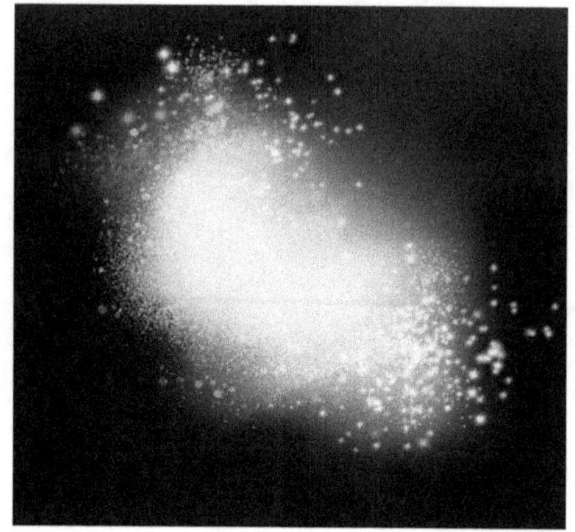

# #UNTITLED

This love
was once
the oasis
you ran to
during the dark
moments
that
scarred
your heart
to fear
the light...

# #A BEAUTIFUL DEFEAT

Your heart
beats of
a story
that your
smile
forgot about...

## #7.7.7

If love
is a gift,
how did I get so lucky?
To give up
on love
only for it
to find me
when I
was


lost...

# #LET.LOVE.LEAD

I don't wish
to be lost,
but without you,
I don't need
a
map...

# #CLOUDNINE

We went in
over our heads
and now
we're stuck in the
clouds...

# #UNTITLED

I was
soul-kissed...

Chasing our
love
was indeed
the sweetest prize,
but you're
the
rarest
of
gifts...

# #RISK TAKER

Whether
you
trust in this or not,
I know
to place
all my bets
on you.

I'd gamble
time
if I had to!

# #PRAY

Do you know what really sucks?
When you pray for change
and change doesn't come.

And you're told to "never lose hope"
time and time again,
but nothing is delivered.

None.

So,
you hold on to hope,
even when it
burns and stings,
leaving scars for some.

We are always so focused on a
specific result
that our desired change
passes by our eyes.

It might not be the change that
we recognize, however we tend
forget the whole feeling
of wanting change,
ceasing to witness that change is alive.

So, you cry in a pity,

with salt water in your eyes.

And now you're sad
and you don't know
why.

But change indeed came,
it arrived,
it just passed you
by...

When we are always so focused on a specific result,
change will appear and pass
right before your very eyes.

You must choose to see it,
change is in motion
at all times...

# #CHERRY

There is nothing
sweeter
than the truth
from lips
that taste
of
bitter
lies...

# #SO, I DID!

And with a kiss
he said:
remember this,
love as if
love was
the sweetest dream
you do not
want to wake
from...

# #UNTITLED

Even at what
she thought was
the end,
lay
another
beginning...

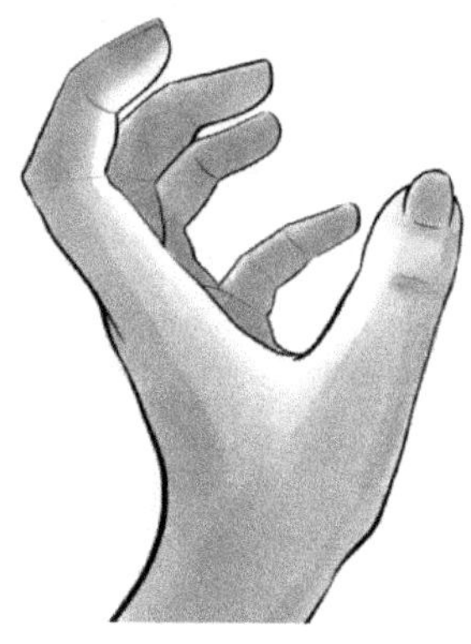

# #GOODBYE REGRET

Why bother with
regret?

When perhaps it was once a wish,
and now it's a fantasy
that came true.

Perhaps I prayed
for you,
just
to lose you
too...

# #FIRE&DESIRE

How awful it
became
when we broke
every promise
and ended
in pieces
beautifully
shattered
all over
the floor,

and still,


wanting more...

# #ASHES TO DUST

I ask that you
do not run
or linger
across my mind.
Even after all
this time,
my mind couldn't
bear
the thought
of
you...
Tongue tied,
my kryptonite,
to these
weary eyes...

# #GROWING PAINS

I loved you,
but I never really knew
it to be true
until the sun one morning
sang,
and I knew
a new beginning
would
commence
because of
you...

Emerging from a world
of darkness
and
into the light,
the day I walked
away from love,
         from you...

# #FEELS

All I
remember
was
numbness,
as
I
held
you
in
my arms
so
tight...

# #SWEET MERCY
## (words unspoken)

And the
tears
flowed
and poured
when I thought
there was a drought,
from a love
that
stole…

Leaving
me
breathless,
with words
untold…

# #WILD BEAST

You are
a world
of chaos
and
I
am
a
thrill-seeker...

# #O.N.L.Y. (GROW)

Trust me with all that
you are.
Allow me to shower
your heart
with a
fruitful love
and a
melody
that lasts
forever...

# #20/20

I always learn the
hard way.
Beautiful eyes
always
come with
beautiful
lies...

# #ANGER
(a freestyle)

Do not destroy a moment of your
happiness for uninvited anger.
It is a guest
that refuses to leave.

It ravishes through your space,
creating debris of the things
that make you "me",
the things that make you free!

Remember your moments of joy
and do away with anger.
You are more than your
feelings,
overcome the void!

# #UNTITLED (PRESENT MOMENT)

We long for
and
enjoy the moments that
only last a second,
but
live on
forever
in us...

# #LOVE IN FULL EFFECT
(unconditional)


And if our story ends,
know that
    love
doesn't...

# #DRY CRY!

It is not just
the lovers who cry;
the one who
thought they were
loved cries the
most...

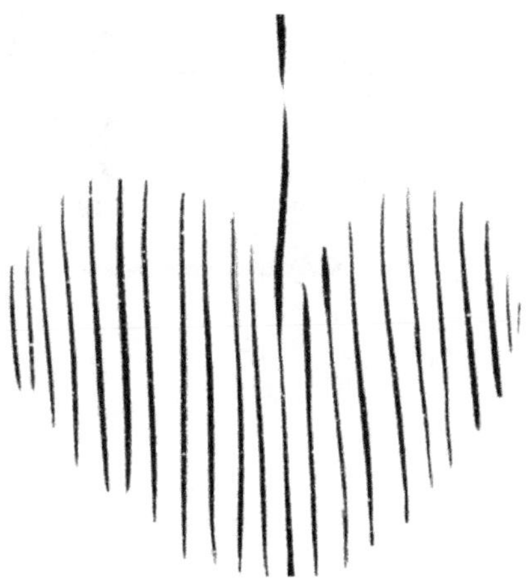

# #BROKEN PIECES (V1)

Love and lust
both
hold
secrets
as ears
we once
felt
we could
trust...

# #GARMENTS OF A BUTTERFLY (PART 2)

I, the butterfly,
and you,
the song
I've never
heard.
A melody not
even sung
among
the rarest
of
birds...
A tune that
my ears
couldn't
unhear
and with this
your intent became clear:
you were looking for a love to drain,
a beautiful distraction became your game.
What a muse—turning my life into pain.
You drew me in
and
I found myself following you into
the nights.
Changing my usual habits
and I grew to
love you too,
but I'll never remember you the same.
Once that tune

stopped,
I saw
the illusion
fade
away
and all that was left:
pity,
me,
and shame,
in a closet
of
self-loathing
blame.

# #HOLLOW MAN

But
I find joy
in the echoes
your words
have left
in the silent spaces
of my mind...

and now I can't
forget you...

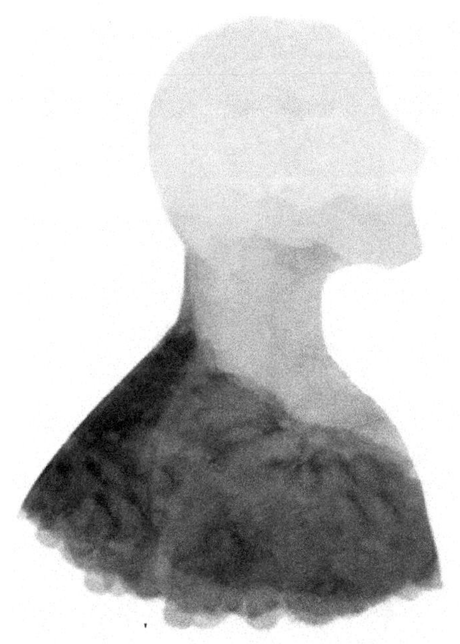

# #HOLLOW MAN (V.2)

And I find joy
in the echoes
of your heartbeat.

I must confess,
it's the pulse
keeping me alive...

# #BROKEN OPEN (V4)

We both
tore
apart
things
that
were
once
never
broken...

# #BLINK

Every day,
I want
to wake
up
with eyes rejoicing
that they are alive!
To open eyes that
expand wide!
Not with eyes
that just
look
alive...

# #MILK & HONEY
## (A Taste of Grace)

I became the mist
in the dreams
that are
most beautiful to you.
One that is
hard to ignore
and
filling the air
with
the softest kisses
water has to offer
on such
a delicate face...

# #DANTE'S INFERNO

Life
is a series
of no ends.
A multitude
of trying
again.
Beginnings
on repeat,
agains and agains,
knowing
no
end...

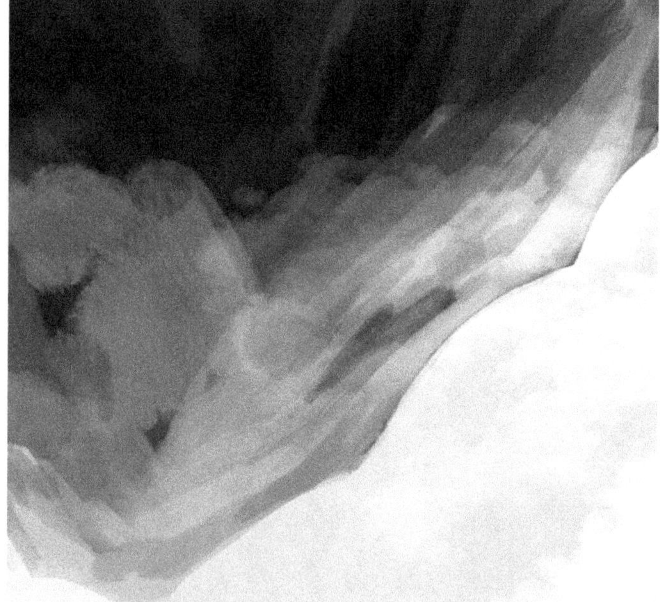

# #AQUA

All it takes is
one breath
to become
breathless
around you...

# #STEADY

No need to rush.
Catch your breath
in a love
like this...

# #FUN HOUSE

We may be either stuck
or broken.
Truth is,
we brought ourselves
through doors
we've opened,
leading to more doors
where there
was no turning back.
To only more doors
distorting the facts.
So, now we find
comfort
in the lies
keeping
the illusion
intact...

# #BABAR
(*so selfish*)

You leave
no room
for me,
nor
the
elephant
in the
room...

And if my words
    don't reach you,
    for you,
    I'd write...
For you,
    I'd sing...
For you,
    I'd dance,
    for you,
    I'd create art.
    For you,
    I'd devote...

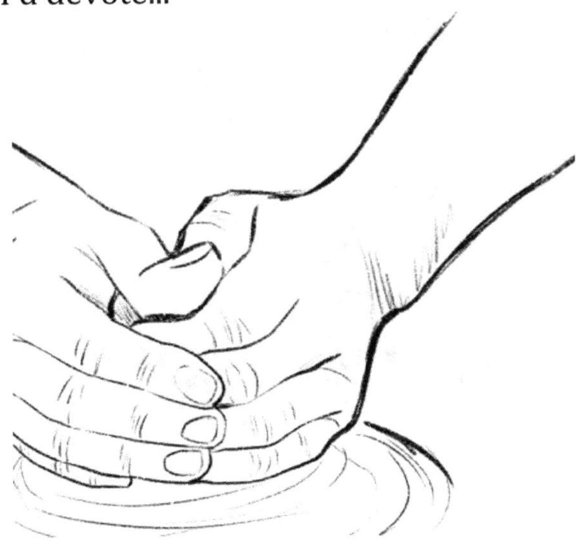

# #UNTITLED

Winners are those
who know
how to deal
with losing.
To navigate after each loss
and to find your way
after each setback,
now that's
winning!

**#9**

You ask,
what does an overdose
on numbness feel like?
It feels like new
heights,
new plights,
the body on the highest verge
of destruction,
while coasting
on its
lowest flight...
An unhealthy fight...

# #INDIGO

I hate
when
there's something to be
said,
but the words
don't appear.
Something to be heard,
but
only falls
upon
deaf
ears...

# #SWEET OBLIVION

You were a sweet
delusion.
A fantasy
    I
wanted
to
be
lost
in..

# #FANTASY

There were dreams
we shared.
They were keeping us
alive,
 distracting us from our
worldly nightmare.

A nightmare of a world,
only made unfair and judgmental.
A world
made to
rip lungs
to pieces
after taking
in
all the
air.
   A
world
made
unfair
for
those
like
us...

# #PRACTICE HONESTY

In a world
where we live to die,
you are the only thing
keeping me alive.
Living for more life
and
dying to
live with you.

*now that's living...*

# #D.Y.I.N.G.

One of the
worst
feelings
is dying
inside
a living
body...

# #2-EYES

And after all our
time, I realized
that life
can only
be understood
halfway through you.
The rest is through
everyone else,
way beyond me
and the partner I
choose as my
spouse.

"Love is universal,"
 I cry!

It is not meant
to be kept
at the demands of
your selfish mouth.

Allow me to spread
my arms and share
my love with all
those who yearn
to dismantle this
drought!

# #EQUIVALENT EXCHANGE

Between everything
    and
nothing,
is where
you'll find
the answer you seek,
as your journey through life
will stream
different colours
of
victory
and
defeat...

# #VIVA FOREVER

I only wonder,
if death is where life
ends,
then we are immortal
because we have
lived many
different
lives...

# #SIXTH.SENSE

Without the light,
there is no you to see.
Without your scent,
there is no aura to breathe.
Without your love,
I will never live,
I may never be free!

Without you

or your presence

here to comfort and

be

with me...

# #THE CRANE

I will fold a thousand paper
cranes
to right the wrongs,
as
I write about
my
sorrow
that prolonged,
and made it's way
onto you...

A thousand cranes
would suffice,
it sure will do!

   To
amount
    to
a thousand paper cuts,
even if it took every day,
until I get back
to when
I lost you...

# #AS BELOW, SO ABOVE

I'm longing for moments
that only
freedom
in the sky can supply and withstand.

I am a dove of light,
made with melanin skin,
kept down below
with no flight plan.

Given a river that reflects a bright blue sky,
carrying a dream in the highest realms
made for these wings of mine.

If only I could fly...

# #NEVER 2 LATE

It is time
that will remove
the stitches from the heart.
It is time
that will open you up
to new inner possibilities,
beginnings,
salvation,
and a chance
    for
a new start...

# #UNTITLED

You,
in the grasp of
my hands
and in close range of my
toes,
I never thought we'd
be here,
so bitter,
so cold.

Rejecting
each other's
souls...

# #DECISIONS YOU HAVE TO DECIDE ON

Decisions are tough pills
to swallow.
Tough swallows
gulping down enormous pain
for one to take.
A decision to influence a lifetime
of regret,
from
just
another
honest
mistake...

# #MANIC

Frigid kisses
covered
with comforting
lies.
Warm memories
lived,
      and finished with
a
lifetime of

demise...

# #UNTITLED

In each hour,
day after day,
she finds herself
with you,
right by your side,
night after night,
but she is alone...

# #GARMENTS OF A BUTTERFLY (V.3)

Wings are a
blessing and
a curse.
You fly,
but at the same time,
you can plateau at a level
of comfortable flight.

Sometimes you may soar at
an unknown height,
where you're below the stars
and unable to see the sky.

And when looking down,
all that appears is
strange nothingness,
and yet,
still captivating
to the eye...

# #UNTITLED

Becoming many things,
living very different lives,
experiencing all the earth
has to offer,

and aiming for

  the moon,
beyond

sunrise.

# #RIGHT DIRECTION

And judging
where
the wind
blows,
sometimes you're lost,
and other times,
you're
free...

# #PERFECT ACCIDENT

Your lips call it fate,
but deceit was the host.

It was loneliness covering
the ugliest of things,

the things only
the mirror
sees
most...

# #NO TEARS

The rain was no
match for the tears
that she poured.
The ocean
grew envious of the waves
her eyes
had stored...


A woman,
with a strength only resilience can define,
beautifully dragging her sorrows across the sand,
across the shore,
searching for the path
where the stars align
once more...

# #EMBER

And he loved
the only
star in the sky that night...
How beautiful it is to be alone
sometimes and
shine...

# #USED TO

We used to run with
the wind,
now you just suck up
all the air.
Never playing fair...

# #ELEMENTAL LOVE

There is a beautiful
storm
brewing
inside of you.
I want
all that
fire
 and
rain...

# #7 DAYS

Today is all we have.
Embrace me now
and into
tomorrow's
morning
sun...

# #SOUL FOOD

Half of you
is all
I need
to
feel
whole...

# #PENPROPHET (V.2)

And blindly
he said to all,
there
is only one cure,
and that is to see
the beauty
in all things...

And so,
the people could
see again...

# #STREET WALKER

I walked the earth
on a sidewalk
that took me in
no clear direction.
I gave myself to faith
to guide me
and it delivered me
into the hands of
deception's
         affection...

# #STAND TALL

To stand for something—now
that's poetic.

To stand for nothing—now
that's pathetic!

# #4 LIFE

**Why do you bother trying?**

Me: Because I want to be
by your side
and enjoy
every
moment
calling you darling.
To see you every morning,
so you die knowing
a love that nurtures
even after mourning.

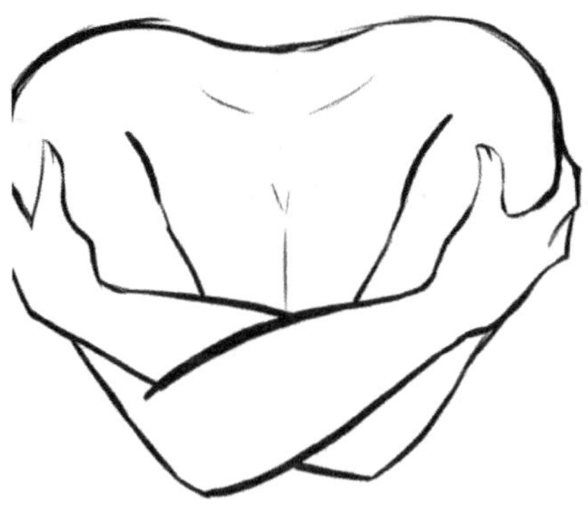

A love that
never fails
to deliver...

# #LOVE DEEP
(heartless)

We always
use lips
that
they can taste,
for
a love
   that
they can
never feel...

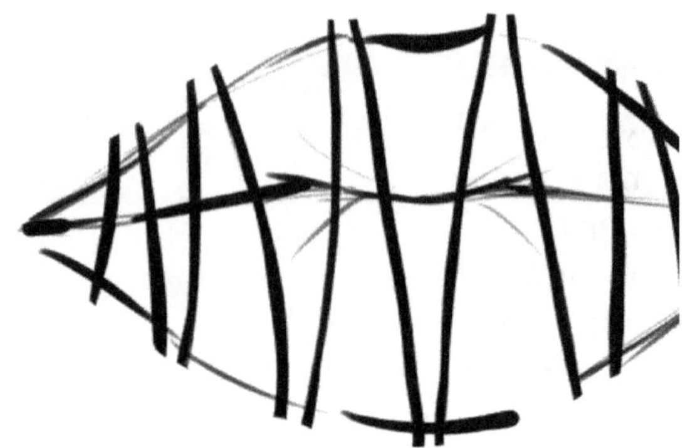

# #LIFE

A dead heart is a
life waiting to be
lived.

Look alive.
Be alive.
Live alive.

# SALVATION

# #PRACTICE DETACHMENT

Sometimes
the most loving
thing we can do/
is to love things
less.

Let us detach,
not obsess.

Everything fades child,
until

there's nothing left...

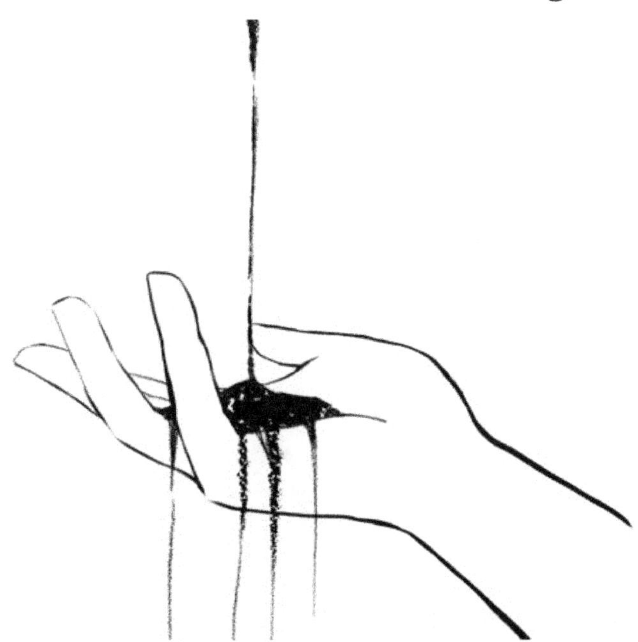

# #S.A.L.U.T.E.

The only healing
left
for one
of us to achieve,
is the one
where
one
of us
leaves...

# #CATHEDRAL

Chase your demons away.
Know that angels
are
always
near...

# #NIGHT WHISPERS

She
whispered,
*"love is the
future"*
and he held
out his hand...

# #MONOLINGUALISM

In a room full of strangers,
we found a common
language
when our eyes communicated

one word:

*-everlasting...*

# #YOUR EYES
(home is where the EYES are)

It was in those
pretty eyes,
I felt
I could get
lost in,
and still
find my
way
back
home...

# #UNTITLED

You can't go
back to the way
you used to be.
The present moment
is still,
but it also
moves forward,
so move where
you want to be.

And take time to enjoy along the way.

Imagine the
possibilities
and
you will see.

A new you,
made whole,
made true!
A living
testimony
living
through
you!
      Who knew!

# #HOPELESS@MOST

Hopelessness bites,
but I'm not worried,
for I know
hope is the
antidote
for the venom
that
hopelessness
recites...

# #UNTITLED

Our goodbye
was
a sweet
beginning...

**#INDIFFERENT**

We live in the
shadows.
Allowing for
the masses
to decide:
how to live,
what to hold dear,
how to be.
Unfairness,
simply given out
as a byproduct of fear,
for folks
seen as
'other'
among
        peers...

*shhh...I'm evolving...*

# #EVOLVE

I hope you can
find it
in your heart
to follow
that melody,
that tune,
because I did
and it
led me
away from you
to
myself...

# #ROBYN
(step 1)


How do you
get over
a lover?

You jump.

And the rest begins there...

# #UNTITLED

The heart whispers
words
in every beat
to those
who choose
    to
listen...

# #100 HEALING

There's a pain that comes
with resistance.

There's a pain that comes with
forgiveness.

Necessary.
Vital.
Accept.
Reflect.
Surrender.

Walk with intent,
breathe with intent,
see with intent,
be with intent...

# #JACKLYNN AND THE BEAN STALK

So many
dead
flowers
in her
garden,
but she continues
to plant
and
she grows,
beautifully...

# THE EXCERPTS

# #FINESSE DA VINCI
(Part 2)


We were far
from the truth,
nowhere near what was real.

It was deception at most,
conceited lies
and topped with a selfish toast.

It was open hearts
faced with no way in.

Hopeless,
before anything
could begin...

# #HEAR, SEE NO EVIL

Read my heart
and
not the lies
coming
from
these
lips...

# #1000 PRAYERS

Prayers,
for that one day to arrive,
as we hope and wish,
and patiently wait
for that moment of bliss.
But the further
that one day becomes,
the day we wait for,
eventually becomes
FOREVER,
and my unanswered
prayers are left in the
sky with no resolve,
and I spend my day
waiting on a time
that is
far gone.

One day, one day, one day,
they say,
but they don't warn that one day
may not happen right away,
and the wait,
lives on forever
and time fades with
no results at all.

One day,

one day,

one day,

they say…

but will one day come?
Or will it forever stay away?
I ask.
One day,
they say,
you'll find the answer that way.
So, I wait…

# #SPEAK!

They say,
there
is a sweet spot
in love,
 and
there,
you
will find a
language
made up of
never-ending unconditionality.

*Don't stop talking...*

# #NARA

You ask,
what does
love taste
like?

-The day we met.




*The sweetest day.*

# #SEEING RED

They drew blood.
Only because they loved
this hard.
Gore-red,
was the only colour
left to prove,
through their relationship
blues,
and thick
coloured
        tears...

# #INTERGALACTIC

What does the galaxy and
you have in common?

- A whole universe.

**#DRY CRY**
(version 2)


Why cry?

Me: Because
you fail to see
these eyes...
So,
I let
my roar
vibrate on your
heart strings instead,
since your ears
are
desensitized...

# #UNTITLED

If pain is the teacher,
then
      love
 is
the master...

# #WARMTH

I find an eternal
smile,
when our eyes
lock
with a love
that
doesn't know of
a frown.

Drowning in your lips
&
breathing in sync,
in the warmth of
our
kiss...

# #UNTITLED

Make me care
some more.
Sitting on a mountain of empty
kisses I've stockpiled
from the ceiling to the floor.
I simply reject lips that
are lacking
substance from the kisses
that they offer.

I simply reject the kisses
that don't come with something
real!

I hate empty kisses
that only stick to the
skin,
but come
and
feel of
nothing
from
within!

# #UNTITLED

You were a special kind,
my
"favourite"
kind.
The
kind that
exists
outside of
fleshly
desires
and
man made
concepts such as
time.

You
were
special.
A special kind.

You
existed in
your own
right and
to be seen
by you
was all I
needed
to be
selective
with what
I call
      mine...

# #ACQUIRED TASTE
(version 2)


I was a mistaken bit.
A puzzle in the mix.

Another painful
rejected bite
on the lips
of lovers
seen unfit,
with eyes
that look past pupils,
and a tasteless
aftertaste in the pit
of my appetite.

Oh, the things I crave.

Silly me,
for always wanting more...

# #UNITED

We looked up to the sky and she asked,

where do thunderclouds go
after the rain?

Me: We carry them with us.

# #SEE YOU NEXT FALL

You blossomed,
while
life appeared to be dying
all
around.
And when the skies turned
to grey,
and the leaves fell
to the ground,
from the spring
dew to the fall
nights,
remember
this
love doesn't
change like
the seasons...

# #CRAZY.SEXY.

Crazy,
without knowing me,
we thought this would last
a lifetime.
Crazy,
but by speaking,
our word grew a bond too.
Crazy how the heart works.
Sexy,
that we would be together,
crazy, I know,
but true.
Crazy,
to think I saw a life with you,
and I know you saw it too.
But, I didn't see that things would
erupt like so,
crazy,
        we didn't have a clue...

**#X**

I'm a sea
of wonder...

Get lost
or set
sail.

To
pursue
disaster
or seek a treasure
in hopes that you'll
prevail...

You see,
to be lost at sea,
only comes with mystery,
and a life in limbo,
in jeopardy.

Are you willing to set sail
and get lost with me?
On a journey into
oblivion,
a beautiful epiphany.
*You + me.*

# #YOKO

Ocean child,
tell me of the places
where you hide,
the places
where you cry.
Tell me where I can find
the purest you,
where the waves of your voice only
speak truth,
and I will listen to the message
carried in your words
and believe
them
to be true...

# #1/2

We may not be whole right now,
but what
we
have
are
two
halves...

made whole.

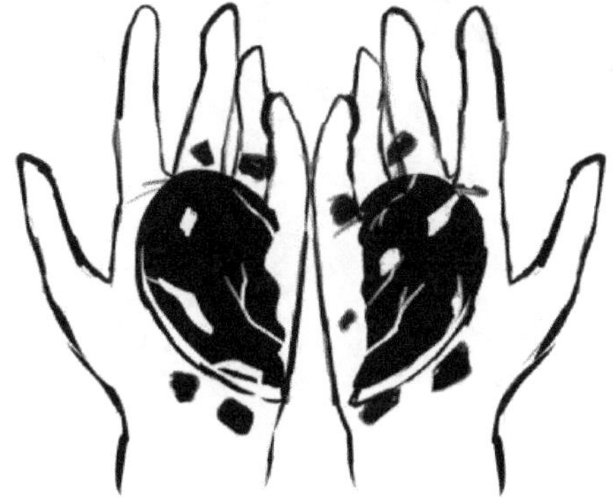

# #UNTITLED

I want
to be
beside you,
even on
the loneliest
of nights...

## #DESTINY

In my pain,
I'm still holding you.
Filling
buckets
of disappointment
and
floating on rivers of
tears down the
melancholy
streams and corners
of my heart's ravine...

If only this poem
was half
as
captivating
as
you...

# #LIMBO

In these bits
and pieces
of every poem,
you'll find
the sorrows that
I swept.
The guilt that
I kept.
A heart expanding
and closing
to life's constant
beautifulness
and beautiful
mess...

# #UNTITLED

You knew me,
but you didn't know
how to love me...
You held me,
but you didn't know how to hold me...
You were there,
but
  I
already
realized
that
  I
found
comfort
in your
absence...

# #GOODBYE

It wasn't love, it was patience at most.
Perseverance.
A friend to confide in.
Not a lover
for a life together on cloud nine.
We never got the chance to float!
It was short-lived, a sweet moment,
a bitter farewell,
topped with a
final toast.

The sweetest goodbye
came from such a tragic
disaster.
I found better days; I assure you.
Filled with more laughter!

# #UNTITLED

Honor the light in you,
it's the pieces that shine too bright
to see!
Feel the light in you,
it will widen your vision
to clearly see!

# #ANDTHENUCAME

He was addicted
to a cold heart
by the moonlight,
before it was torn.

Now it sits,
idle,
alone.
It is the calm before the storm.
A heart beating
will
inevitably
have to
mourn...

# #UNTITLED

Kid: "what's life?"
Me: healing and breathing...
Life is being alive,
moment to moment,
feeling to feeling..."

If there's one thing I know
for certain,
it's that
trying your best
doesn't end just
the one time you
tried...

Trying your best looks different every time.

The path
to greatness
starts on the hands and knees.
Greatness is only worthy
for those who
never
quit...

Who knew the bottomless pit
and paved the way to the top,
until
the sweat turned sweet.

A commitment
with no end,
never succumbs
     to
defeat.

I am whole.
I am complete.
I am everything
that I want to be.
In this moment,
I am whole,
all possibilities
and
infinities
exist
within
me...
I am whole.
I am complete.

# #GIVER/GIVING TREE

I AM A GIVER.
Carrying the weight,
the burden.
Keeping the walls up.
I am a giver.
No needing,
no receiving,
just giving for
those who
love receiving.
I am a giver.
I have grown in my role,
and accepted that
as the giver,
I carry the cross,
I carry the tow.
I bare witness that as a giver,
this is the only sacrifice
made left for me to grow.

I am a giver.
My destiny is
in service of others,
in hopes that I may
fill my soul and full potential,
even if
it is not my wish, not my will,
I am a giver,
destined to fulfill.

There's a void
deep inside of me
reflecting
the pit of my soul.
Reflecting
darkness of round eyes,
behind lids half closed.
There's no telling
to the depths
of where it goes...

A hole made inside
the realm of
my existence
that I sink into

*and it swallows me whole.*

The moment to renew
is always one decision
away.
So remember, throughout the day,
you can
become a clearer,
stronger,
better,
you!

I put you through it...
The work became tough.
And by doing that to you,
I put myself through it too...

- work is never done (2 Much)

We are the
things
we
keep in
our grasp,
so
I held
you
closer...

-complete [my reflection]

Forever
never
tasted
so good,
when we sealed
lips.
Locked in a fate
where the only
'forevers',
are
moments of
bliss.

Eternity,
captured
in a kiss...

The birth to
A thousand sparks
began
with the first
light...
The first spark
was able to
light
the rest of the path,
guiding the way
out of the
dark...

Chasing moments is not living,
but to bathe,
bask,
in all it has
to offer,
now that's
LIFE.

*-process*

When I started speaking,
I learned so much.
I heard my voice
for the first time...

*-untitled*

If there's one
thing
that I
know for certain,
it's that
the only way
out
is through…

Human beings
are strange creatures
indeed...
We run
from the light
when it is
almost
always our saviour,
our grace,
oftentimes,
what we need...

*-healing*

Only
a real
lover
deserves you
at your best.
They always know
how to lay
to rest
the walls
we put up,
filled with oppositions
we call
"tests"

*-risk*

Life is suffering
and beautiful chaos
at the same time.
And then there's you,
a realm
of balance…

It isn't the silence
nor the petty lies
that bother me,
it was the
"I love you".
The greatest lie ever told.

Do-Ray-Mi,
you played
me
like a symphony,
beautifully out of tune...

*-scales*

I still say
little prayers every time
I pass by
our spot,
wondering if you do the
same.
Do the memories
flood
your brain
as it does mine?

-*where we met.*

I vowed to never
forget you
and
yet,
you're off
making
new
memories…

I went into it
with a raw heart,
the purest of intentions from
the start.
I dropped all walls and facades,
I went in being vulnerable,
stripping naked and uncovering
all of my flaws.

I went in so sure,
feeling special
and convinced that
it was worth it all,
so pure.
That I could stand tall,
and we could be together,
but then came the fall.

We were just growing into it, just to fall out of it...

*Love.*

May you remember to
abandon all of your troubles
at the door,
before you begin
to love
all of mine...

*-selfless*

I was determined
to see myself through!

Let me remind you
that
I am made of
the strongest of cloths,
not fabrics
that have been
reused.

Broken attracts
what it looks like.
They find comfort
in their ugliness
and warmth
in ways
of coping.

*-bonding*

I know
I pulled
away,
but so did you.
The grass always looks
greener in the opposite
direction,
compared to the crops
we've destroyed.

*-communal gardening*

And when
the fire burns
out,
it's that
look,
that
stare,
that we never forget.
Imprinted on our psyches for life,
when we see them
for the first time
in the dark.

*-ember* (version 3)

I restarted
with you,
and ventured
on a journey that
I've been on before.

But I kept quiet,
because you felt life,
and lived it for the first time,
and I couldn't take
that from you,

so,

I watched instead...

*-sidelines*

I found
my talk,
and I found the words,
I then found my walk,
but I'm voiceless and
lost
around you.

*-lost & whisper*

When it comes to love,
I always try to choose the lesser
poison,
but I learned
it's fatal
all the time...

I am beyond

what you remember of me
and
I have surpassed
even my own
expectations...

*-SOAR*

I remember how much
I hated you,
us,
after we split.
Love is a spectrum
and
hate is on the
other end of it.

And that's when I knew...

*-true(L)*

I'm in a really
good place now,
with an amazing view.

*-me&you*

I knew
it was bad,
before it felt good.
There were days
I would run to you
with open arms,
knowing the danger
that awaits.
But, you take my pain away,
this, I knew,
but you're bad for me, it's true.
I refuse to believe
the cause of my demise,
was a dangerous love battle
with you…


*-untitled*

But this is goodbye.
I picked up all my mistakes,
with all of my might,
and
I never looked back.
The weight
was the price for the future
I longed for.

*-freedom*

I drink from my own source,
that's the secret.

So much
  so
that you
cannot deny
I am
an
unstoppable force.

-inner core

# #EVERLASTING

I promised
U
I'd wait,
but
when eternity
came,
you
were
gone...

It was in that moment
when I stopped listening
to what I think I should hear,
it was then,
right there,
when I heard it...

*-silent voice*

## #K9

And I know you'll never call me,
but I know
I'm on your mind,
you said you'd
love me forever,
to lengths
undefined.
Now,
I'm sitting alone
with this bottle
thinking
about
the times...

# #AJOURNAL4WANDERERS

Lost.
A beautiful lost soul,
never tired or fearing
of getting old.
Living with eyes wide
open
and soaking up moments
and sensations life offers,
from the ground felt
from the soles
of our feet.
Making us feel whole,
a part of something greater,
complete.
A part of a collective,
even when we feel lost,
distraught,
And at times broken down
by defeat.

Beaten down countless
times,
removing our gentleness
and beauty every single
time,
before we could even say
stop, please!

Because we are different
and when we move

around spaces
across different eyes,
one thing stays the same,
the glare.

Looking at something
they cannot understand,
nor explain or identify,
a foreign soul with vicious
eyes are the worst,
casting judgement upon
those who are different,
unwelcoming and
simply unfair!

# #FOOL'S GOLD

Your heart was the prize,
while my heart was the
sacrifice.
I played my cards
carefully and wise,
but I lost myself
by vowing to love you
into the afterlife.

Your smile led me to
places where your dark
dimmed my light,
and the lies held me
airtight,
breathless, by the way
you
stole all of my might.

Weak to my knees,
knowing all along
I was just a pawn,
invaluable to you.
A treasure you never
kept
for long...

# #BLUEHEART

Beyond measure is where
you will find me.
I am not made for any one person,
but I am beautifully made
to be set free.
Unrestrained.
Unattainable.
That's me.
Even if I am what you
wished or prayed for,
I am not your blessing.
I exist beyond even your
deepest fantasies,
I am beyond what your
mind can even perceive
of me,
so how could you
possibly desire me,
without understanding
me,
or
even being capable of
defining me?

How can you love what
cannot be named!
How can you love
someone that bares such a
unique pain?
You must continue

on your way,
alone,
I cannot be tamed,
I am made for no man,
But I am beautifully made,
to be set free.
Alone.
Not something to gain...

# #ROSE

Satisfaction,
as my eyes daze into yours.
For days and hours,
heaven sent,
as I carry you
across the most beautiful
plain of flowers!
Together forever,
your love,
for mine,
equals
ours...

# #UNTITLED

Without fear,
there is no courage.
Without death,
there is no life!
Without imperfection,
there is no truth!

Peace be with you
&
peace be on your way,
but they never cautioned
of places where peace
would not be
an invited guest
to stay...

# RISING

# FIN